Clinically Naked

Photos by:
James F. Lyons Photography

Afterword Press

ISBN: 978-1-952555-09-1

Clinically Naked

A Collection of Poems

By

Cédes Ascensión

A Special Dedication to

My husband, Stephen, who always encouraged me to put my pen to paper.

All of the people that produced conversations and experiences in my life that brought forth my ambitions as a writer.

May my transparency allow you to know that circumstances always have the ability to improve, but you must allow it.

Table of Contents

Chief Complaint

Hide and Seek

Once, she was like a nickel
Smooth edges and all.
Everyday past five
Came down on her like leaves in fall
A simple game of hide and seek,
Over two decades ago still makes her weak
Four kids playing together, innocent it seemed
Until the four were split in twos, you and her on the same team
You filled yourself behind closed doors
While the wide eyed little girl had fear seeping through her pores
There were skeletons in your closet
They were her bones, clothed with her flesh and no one ever saw it
Defenseless, she laid motionless across your lap
With no hesitation, you commenced the attack
She remained quiet as you signaled her not to make a sound
It felt like an eternity waiting to be found
You inhaled deeply, getting high off of her smell
Each moment, mentally, she retreated further into a shell
Twenty plus years later, her story she will exclaim
It's long overdue. She's ready to rid herself of this pain
She wants to forgive, but she doesn't think she can
You enrage her, you disgusting excuse of a man!
All this time you've been living scotch free
Well, step aside. You've got to the count of three
She's liberating herself. Now it's HER you should fear
She's thirty now, all woman, and this is her year
I wish you well in jail, hell or therapy
Maybe there you can share that this little girl was me

Rey

I was just a teen
The day I stumbled onto a horrific scene
I struggled for the words to find
The visions immediately burned scars onto my mind

The 911 operator couldn't understand what had happened
She asked me to slow down, take a breath and count to ten
It was then I told her that my brother was hanging from a rope
face purple, rope wrapped tightly around his throat

She said I had to cut the rope, that I had to go back in
I cried NO! I couldn't stand to see that all over again
She explained that seconds were important, that he might still have an ounce of air
That I had potential to save him before help got here

Trembling I cut and screamed. As he fell, his knees did not bend
It was then I was certain that his life had come to an end
His body fell over causing a loud thud
As he went down, he hit the wall, smearing his own blood

Just me and my shadow as I ran to open the front door
The police had arrived. I wasn't alone anymore
I had to notify my parents. One more call to make
This was all too much. How much more could I take?

I dial up my mom and ask her to please come home
She tells me to hang on as she gets my dad on the phone
My knees buckled as I told him Rey was dead. He's no longer here
There is no response, only the sound of the phone dropping from his ear

I feel a heaviness as I stare out of the window
The coroner is outside. The neighbors now know
For the last thirteen years I've wished that things had happened differently
I've questioned why you? Why me?

Since I can't erase what occurred that day
I aim to push forward. There is no other way

Self-Talk

"Why can't you do anything right?
Everyday you're getting closer to the psych ward."

I'm just looking for the silent way out.
But it doesn't quiet the voices; in my head they shout.

My mind is on fire 212 degrees
Strange thoughts set ablaze float like embers in the breeze.

100 percent attention is never enough.
Put on your seatbelt, this road is about to get rough.

My consciousness drifts too often in the clouds.
And when they find out, they'll run off in the crowds.

"I can't blame them if that's what they'd do
Cause I'd do the same with a crazy mess like you."

Call a therapist. She needs some assistance.
On second thought; put on the straight jacket without resistance.

Be real, if I let my insanity hang would you walk away
Or brace yourself and accept me this way?

"What's wrong with you? Is it a chemical imbalance?
Or is this one of your so-called multi-personality talents?"

"I'll tell you one thing, you're not fooling me."

Anchor

Coming up with absolutely any reason
To stop dealing with a mended heart for one more season

I hurt myself too much with you
I lost myself in an ocean of things so untrue

Sitting in a corner, barely dealing with anhelation
All due to this anxiety stricken mentation

Tired of stuffing the negativity away in a drawer
I won't stand to live like this anymore

Struggling to make things right
Surely tired, but not enough to give up this fight

I've got my eyes on the prize, that beautiful oasis
Paddling onward to get where that place is

I don't know about you, but I'm swimming out to my ship
In hopes that while I'm swimming, I'll become better equipped

Confessions

Do you remember being told not to have sex,
But you went and did it anyway?
Yeah, yeah. Go ahead and lie.

We'll sit here and be honest about the healed parts
But pass the cup on being transparent
When we're currently wrestling with something on our hearts.

So walk with me. Twenty plus years back.
Being young and dumb,
You know the rest.

We called ourselves being safe.
I guess this time it wasn't.
In the midst of things we discover a break.
Except it's not the good kind.

So I ran down to Kaiser.
Mind racing off the pavement
I'm in luck for a Plan B.
It was a close call. Until it wasn't.
A couple of weeks later and a missed period
Meant a frantic plan c.

This wasn't supposed to happen!
Dead in my tracks.
Have you ever been at the cross road
Of "it's either you or me?"

One of us has to go.
I had one major person to lean on and no,
It was not the father.
He was busy dropping dollars on his shoes and clothes.

Do you remember how hard I cried at the clinic
When the results showed two lines?
Many missed days of junior year
How did I mess this up so bad?!

I was terrified.

I had to come up with a plan
Have you ever had to discreetly pick up the pace
So no one would notice the sick look on your face
And to top things off, quietly vomit?
I hid a lot.
Not only my waistline.
I hid my turmoil, my appointments,
Ultrasounds and documents too.

I pushed the limit.
Months went by and…I finally broke;
I pulled the trigger.
It wasn't a smoking gun,
Yet it didn't change the fact that I was still a killer.

I cowered in terror.
I couldn't face my consequences.
In the end, I chose my life
If you can even call this living.

It's been a mixed bag of emotions
Filled with jagged memories.
I'd say thank you, but it's twisted you see.
Because you helped me with a crime I committed 20 years ago
And the only people that knew, were the ones that helped me flee.

Fast forward to July 30, 2020
And I couldn't help but think,
This was my punishment.

I caused this!
I didn't create the life I aborted.
My creator had to mold me into something better
Not just less distorted.
So I had to be completely destroyed.
Violently thrown onto the wheel.

The creation I loved more than anything
That like a balloon inflated me with joy, popped.
My soul exploded into uneven wrinkly
Fragments never to be the same

Call me Ezra.
I could have torn out my hair.
The very air I breathe was snatched
And converted into moments of silence
As my heir left my grasp.

Returned to Sender

I can't say that I ever dreamed of you
Never yearned for this like some women do
Once I learned you were coming though,
One phrase: life changing!

One moment to the next, it became apparent
In the discovery that I would be a parent
That a love like this could not be imagined
Not in my wildest dreams, could I have ever fathomed
That I could fall head over heels like this

No idea of your personality or traits
Not yet a glimpse of a smile or touch
I could hardly wait to hold and kiss you
And gaze into your eyes and at your little face

As you grew, so did my desire to nestle you in my arms
The daily alerts of progress brought forth a song
I keep falling in love with you over and over and over and over again.
I drew pictures in my mind
Imagining your smile, your laugh and even your belly button

Mommy's resilience. Daddy's intelligence
Combined deadset humor
We were going to be in for a treat
Due date, hurry up and get here!
Never had I wanted time to move faster so we could finally meet

How would we adorn your room? Soft colors? Peter rabbit?
Being familiar with stats, we did not begin to nest
Being familiar with God, we shared to those close to us
And knew we would stay prayed up for the best

All too soon we learned that your plans were different than ours
Expecting to see you in a few months
But your time was marked for a different hour
The sparkle in my eyes quickly turned into floods

As the doctor confirmed that was on the screen
Had developed into a nightmare from a dream

The once strong heartbeat described as a flutter
Was no more and I….. was no longer a mother

In less than a minute so much had changed
I had three things to choose from and neither was your name
Instead, three options on how to remove your remains

All that I fantasized about was gone in a blink
Too much to process or even clearly think
Now to go home to break the news and hearts
Not that our baby was a girl or boy
But that today our baby's life had come to a halt

You came to do so much in so little time
Me and your dad became closer to each other and our faith
You answered prayers and questions
For the first time ever I experienced such a love sublime

There is a huge list of things you stand for
Your imprint is so large
This is the greatest blessing and devastation all in one thus far
Your meaning runs deep, just check out your place holder name
RTS. Not only your initials, but a message from your lender

Raphael T. Sharpe, I know you're in great hands
Because you've Returned To Sender.

Devil on My Heels

You enjoy it when I'm in agony
You remind me of my past misery
You would like me to keep you company
But you can't have me. Not now. Not ever

You wallow in creating sadness
You aim to encourage madness
You lurk in the night engulfing those you find into your darkness
But you can't have me. Not now. Not ever.

You work hard on my soul to minify
You call on my mistakes to magnify
You push me to follow your lies
But you can't have me. Not now. Not ever.

Believe & follow Him, He will provide for your every need
Call on Him at all hours, He will take heed
There will be many that try to hinder His lead
But He won't let you have me. Not now. Not ever.

Repent of your sins and He will forgive
There is no other that can top what He gives
What lurks in the darkness does not want you to eternally live
But He won't let you have me. Not now. Not ever.

There is an owner of my soul when my body expires
To walk on His road He inspires
For eternal life and happiness He aspires
And guess what? He won't let you have me. Not now. Not ever.

Evaluation

Pieces

Picking u**p** fragments
Broken by l**i**es
Jagged **e**dges
Emotions **c**rumbling
Mangled dr**e**ams
Sharpened **s**enses

Excommunicado

She is done. Yes. Done.
No time for another opportunity. Not another wolf.

She doesn't care what the next in line is faking to the table.
Tired of the just short of stable,
One to three months' worth of falsified qualifications type of brother.
She's not interested in seeing what you've got on paper
Not interested in you getting the position because "getting your foot in the door"
Is not quite on her ideal list of what she's looking for.

Serious inquiries only.
Underqualified need not apply.
She is ready to be the female praying mantis.

So what is he so afraid of?

He says she keeps her house clean
She pays for all of her things
He says she cooks up a storm
So what is he so afraid of?

He says she works a hard nine to five
She pays her mortgage and all of her bills on time
He says she helps the community in many shapes and forms
So what is he so afraid of?

He says she takes care of her mother and father
She often puts others needs before hers
He says she spills over with love and minimal scorn
So what is he so afraid of?

He says for her goals she is driven
She jumps on the opportunities she is given
He says to self-improvement she has sworn
So what is he so afraid of?

He says with her, he is experiencing things he has never felt
She is the most understanding person in which he has ever dealt
He says time with her is never worn
So what is he so afraid of?

Your words? Or someone else's?

How is it that you claim, claim all that you claim,
But treat me the same as all of those you've run game?
You expect me to feel different today
After using a line on me that you heard yesterday
Words written to you, you pass off as your own and give them to me
I've never felt so damn empty
And now you want to make me feel guilty when you are the one
Baby, honest mistakes are all that I've done
You say that for you I am queen, I am all that you dream
Then why can't you even come up with your own scheme?
Watching tears fall out of my eyes. You don't know what to do when you hear me cry
But it is a must that you feed me lies.
Tell me. Just tell me. You're making my body shake. Spill it. You've already made my heart ache
At least have the courage to unveil your garbage. You won't make my spirit break
This does hurt badly; I can barely make a sound
Almost as if I'm fighting myself to keep my feelings underground
You do and say all that you please. Painful words slip out of your mouth with ease
Burns so deep I drop down to my knees. I gave you the side of me, I'd let no one else see
Someday I'll thank you for making me strong. For people like you, I've dealt with for too long
You'll inspire me to write new lyrics. I am ready for a new song.

Silly Me

I was foolish, head deep in the sand
I expected YOU to show me where I stand
I awaited to be handed this hypothetical place
A place in which I always won the race

Desperately longing for self-realization
Yet, constantly seeking it through external validation
Wondered why my self-esteem was crumbling apart
While searching for acceptance everywhere EXCEPT within my heart

Battling for love on command
Having not yet learned to love MYSELF as I am
Struggling for you to love me on MY terms
Inadvertently filling my own can of worms

Growing tired of crystal tears dropping to shatter
Something has to change. Something that truly matters
Putting aside the material goods
As they'll never get me where I should

Pushing myself to set limits and boundaries
In the process I will gain new and true enemies
Learning to establish a self-check system
Realizing my gifts AND faults and taking time to list them

Practicing validation of my own thoughts and feelings
Rather than taking on what others are dishing and dealing
Taking time to reconcile with my foes
Simultaneously forgiving myself and curing old woes

Slowly plucking out bad weeds
Replacing each one with multiple good deeds
Before you know it, I'll love who I am
Now I know, now I will, now I can

SINGLE

"What's wrong? What happened? Why are you single?" They ask
I'm finally facing myself and trust, it is no simple task
I'm working on what matters; the issues that start within
I could no longer handle running on fumes, it was wearing me thin
Adding an extra piece before it's needed will guarantee that I lose
That is why, for now, it is best that I be without. That is what I choose
When I'm ready, I'll be looking for a man not a boy
I am a woman, not a toy
And when I get there, I'll go in with all of my chips
I'll be done with games and serve my half in a solid relationship
Too many people jump in before they're ready.
Me? Well, I'm learning. Although slow, I'm moving forward. Slow and steady.

Still, I Stand

He carves me continuously
Into something I thought I'd never be
What is he carving? I don't exactly know
But his work on me started long ago

The precise year of my first trial I don't recall
I must have been about five or six
Exposed to the raw pain of sexual abuse
REALLY? WHY does this even exist?

At that age his work, by me was not understood
Years went by of sweeping things under the rug
Instances where I think I didn't remember
Others where I nearly drowned in tears any time that I would

As I got older, I started to date
Becoming a prime target for those that could manipulate
I was confused and didn't know what to make of it
Maybe I believed that I deserved to be in toxic relationships

My first long term boyfriend
Was an athlete, easy on the eyes
My low self-esteem kept me there
Despite his cheating. Despite his lies

In between all of this YOU'D THINK I'd catch a break
But not yet. For now, I'd get hit with another ton of bricks
At the age of 18, I found my brother lifeless
I must be having a nightmare. SOMEONE. ANYONE! HELP ME WAKE!

I became a prisoner. Trapped in my own body
Never imagined that death would be in the same room staring back at me
That's it! No more! I had hit my limit
Only to discover I had to brace myself because His work wasn't quite finished

It seemed to be one thing after another
Some big. Some small
Each trial breaking me down just a little bit more
Until the point I could not bare to live my life at all

The hour came when I fantasized about suicide
No longer wanting to deal with living
Looking for a place where it didn't hurt anymore
Which way out was all I had to decide

Desperate. I felt I had nowhere to go
It was then that I knew I had reached my ultimate low
And it was then that I knew help was what I needed
I swallowed my pride and for someone to extend a hand I silently pleaded

He sent aid to me in the form of a loving sister
I struggled with opening up, but she SHOWED me
Her life was NOT perfect. She had experienced MORE than her share
Bad relationships, depression, wolves in sheep's clothing had not missed her

Years of therapy came. Not until I crossed the storm did it make sense that Jesus knew
EVERYTHING that I felt
Every tear, every groan. He heard it
My experience was only a tiny fraction of what he was dealt

I'll be honest, the transition was rough and it was NOT overnight
I mean after all, I am human
I bleed. I cry. Problems STILL come into my life
But the truth is, YOU ARE NOT ALONE and neither am I in this fight

He is my strength.
And He is there every time and anytime I call him
He takes care of me BEYOND belief and BEYOND my mistakes
His promises he WILL NOT… CANNOT break.

It wasn't until YEARS after these natural disasters
That I realized weaknesses weave tight bonds.
ALL of God's giants had flaws
My SHARED vulnerability is going to be a part of somebody else's happily ever after

He has so many things in store for you AND me
There isn't anything in my life that isn't his will
Yes, even trials.
And whatever comes I KNOW he will keep my mind and heart still

If you don't already know what he wants of you
Reflect on how you can help others by simply sharing what you're going through
He will go before you, encourage you, mold and heal you
From the beginning of time to the end of time and always on time.

To a Lost Child

Tossing and turning in your bed
Sirens screaming red
How may I aid you?

Your sorrow you cannot disguise
I see the pain in your eyes
Tell me. What do I have to do?

The torment sneaks in through your laughter
It lingers in the air long thereafter
Just say the word and I'll come to the rescue

You've been robbed of your happiness
You did not choose these mountains of mess
But I promise, you are not far from a breakthrough

Sometimes we do not know
Why little ones rebel and away they go
Being a child is difficult, I do not argue

What will it take for us to understand?
Children need more than demands and commands
Pull out a hug. Love is long overdue.

Alternative Medicine

Ocean's Lyrics

Ocean
Salty, loud
Whirling, spinning, pulling
Crashing on the sand, splashing onto toes

Nature's lullabies

Ocean waves crashing
Beautiful alluring sounds
How you comfort me

Rugged Nature

Beautiful rugged pinecone
Having been ripped down from a tree
Free falling to the rubble below
Cracked petals covered in debris
You are such a beautiful creation

Adorned tri-colored tips
Uniquely shaped like a snowflake
No two are exactly the same
Missing pieces from your fall yet standing tall
You are such a beautiful creation

Your multiple layers suit you
To house all of your virtues
Your outer grooves are intriguing
An uneven staircase to your peak
You are such a beautiful creation

Not what you used to be
The ground gave you a different perspective
The work of His hands is apparent
As I marvel over your multiple surfaces
You are such a beautiful creation

If being chopped down by a chain saw,
crash landing to the dirt below
Allowed us to meet face to face,
To admire our flaws and love them
Would you fall for me again?

Autumn Leaf

My colors change
Bright greens to an array of brown hues
So does my texture
Crispy hard from soft, smooth

Not afraid when I fall
I float weightlessly in the breeze
What a beautiful mess I create
When I die and break free

Once clothing twisted branches
Keeping them warm
To tumbling on the pavement
The view is different here, but still I adorn

How my role changes
From dancing carelessly in the wind
To clogging drains
and being swept away into bins

How I long to be back on those tall tree tops

Ladybug

Like a gentle kiss
Approachable
Delicate touch
Youthful

Blinded by beauty
Under construction
Gracefully timid

Wings

Pitter patter
Senseless chatter
What does it all mean?

Beautiful essence
In life's lessons
Even through nightmare filled dreams

Without compromise
Choose truth over lies
Admire yourself you beautiful butterfly

Delicates

I am that delicate garment
The one you must wash gently
Wash me with like colors
Like fabrics, never rugged jeans

Use the baby's laundry soap
You may even need to hand wash me
Never with bleeding colors
Failure to do so may be damaging

Remove me promptly, no twisting
And hang me to dry
Allow the wind and sun to kiss me
As my arms flail on the clothesline

Canvas

Touch me with your bristles
Tell your story on my face
Stain me with your colors
Stroke me with your grace

Whatever your sentiment be
Express it how you perceive
Delve in with true colors
Bold ones if you please

Forests, hills, mountains
You pick your muse
Flick, splatter, brush
Paint upon me how you choose

Black Siren I

Gracefully gliding
Creating surges in the ocean
Oh how she moves

Eyes shining
Like a lighthouse beneath the sea
Illuminating his every move

Timidly watching
Hiding behind the coral
Is he real?

Casting spells
Unknowingly mesmerizing her admirer
Is she real?

Enchanting beauty
Something is different about her
What makes her rare? He wants to know

Seeking daily
To win her heart over
His love he strives to show.

Surgical History

Strong. Rebel. Woman

My name is Araminta Ross
None of you have personally met me
But I'm sure my biography you've read

In 1849 I fled Maryland with a serious cause
You see, I was born a slave
I endured brutal beatings and had a bounty on my head

I left my parents, my siblings and my husband
But I returned at least nineteen times
To help them and hundreds of other slaves flee

You may know me better as Harriet Tubman
Yes, the famous underground railroad conductor
It was my faith in God that saw me through

I never lost fugitives or allowed them to go back
If they didn't believe me
They believed my pistol. I didn't allow for telling of tales

My resistance didn't end with the war
I was a nurse, scout and spy for the Union Government
Because I could move unnoticed, I did

My strength- please remember
My heart -duplicate it as I provided care for many
Respect and dignity- pass it on.

Strong. Rebel. Woman.

Daddy, do you remember?

Daddy, do you remember when I couldn't reach the monkey bars?
You'd pick me up and I'd reach for the stars

Do you remember coming home from your second job everyday?
I'd peel your eyes open as you slept because I wanted you to play

Do you remember taking us on family outings to the beach?
We didn't have a lot but you worked hard to give us all in your reach

Do you remember waking me in the mornings to take me to school?
Reminding me that daddy's girl couldn't settle for a fool

It makes me sad when I remember; heavy tears once I start
Brings me to the reality of present times, in which you are slowly falling apart

There's no turning back time to reverse what life says is due
My heart is crumbling because your life I can not renew

You're replacing daily jogs with a daily dose of medication
And the only promise is that it will slow down the process of deterioration

Science doesn't alleviate my worry. As there is no current cure
I look to the future and it just seems so obscure

Let us pray that your aches and pains go away
Let us be happy and have faith that you'll be more than ok

Daddy, do you remember?

Nanny Harrell

Nanny Harrell
What a great gift I inherited in you.
A first chance to experience
The love of a second grandmother I never before knew.

Quick to spank Stephen to make sure he was treating me right.
Oh how you made me smile.
Didn't know you long enough to witness that left hook
But you jabbed me weekly with love in this short while.

For 83 years, you labored on this earth.
Although some of the lives you touched, we'll never know,
The friends & family you leave behind will miss you
And we'll make sure the good times you created will forever echo.

I will always cherish the day that you
Wouldn't wait any longer
Eager for us to start a new life.
You took our hands in yours
And pronounced Stephen and I, husband and wife.

Although you didn't have the authority
To make our union concrete
I know that you knew it in your heart
And that separate marriage date is now forever bittersweet.

The evidence of love you created
Is living in each of your children & grandchildren
Chips off the old block
Little tidbits of you flourishing in each of them.

I will smile when I think of you.
You've been called from labor to reward
For now you rest.
I know for sure as it is written as God's Word.

Nanny Harrell
I will not say goodbye
For now I say goodnight
Until we meet again, your memory we lift up high.

Bestie

He treats me good
Better than most
Good like a loving friend should

He calls me when I'm ill
Listens when I'm not well
Hugs me 'til the void is filled

His advice fits me like a body sleeve
We can talk for hours on end
He smiles when I laugh and pushes me forth when I grieve

His loyalty is easily admired
He's always there through and through
With no hesitation he runs red lights for me. He truly, simply, inspires

My Chocolate Mocha

Immediate gratification
As I inhale your bitter sweet aroma
Anticipating the richness of your shaved chocolate curls

You are that morning pick-me-up
I can hardly wait to wake
To taste your sweetness on my lips

Enjoying your perfect temperature
Your warming goodness
Travels throughout my body with every sip

There's so much to enjoy
In each and every layer
Simply made to perfection

Mmmm my chocolate mocha

Falling (in love)

If I showed you my flaws
Would you still pause
To reveal your true intentions?
That your cause is not just to
Get into my heart and cash out the equity you've already accrued.

Would you remind me that
Although our time has just begun,
There is no end in sight
There is no price. No need for sales
Because every day that we have is special?

When will I stop treading
So lightly? Keeping in site the
Very instance I trip up, slip up
Rather than being organic
And allowing myself to just fall… in love.

Could I resist the game?
The game that you insist to play
Everyday on my heart
All bets are off unless you are all in
Proving that you don't play unless you play to win.

If I went the distance
And hid the inner me
Down to the very core, nothing else to see
Would your work decline over time
Or would you trickle through my pores slow & steady?

What happens when my thoughts
Are twisted in us?
Completely entangled in this language you speak of
Could you be patient while together
We decode the language of love?

Would you put forth the effort
To prove that what I know
Is not just for show?
That you not only care, but

Truly, genuinely love me?
And since I know what these answers really are
Then just know that you do not stand alone.
That much like you, I am in a zone
There is no need for wishing on a star

Our paths did meet at the fork in the road
I am on this journey for as long as it goes
I understand that you haven't asked yet
But know if you think about asking
The answer is yes.

Outside the Box

Do you remember when we moved into our first place?
Every room was so bare.

Having our first dinner that night was interesting,
Not realizing we were lacking things until the need was there.

The routine of having a meal had been broken.
As the importance of a "simple" dish and glass had come to surface.

Looking back, the beauty of the gifts we received became so real.
Each and every one big and small, as we unboxed them, served their purpose.

Consider a lamp and the need that it meets.
Its creator intended it to produce light.

Now what would happen if it was out of place
And its presence was absent from the night?

There is a light in every one of us.
Each one is personal to one another.

No light is too big or too small
When used to meet the needs of a sister or brother.

My light is mine.
There's something special about it that was given to me,
Individually.

The special assignment
Is to use it collectively.

Unsocial History

Breaking the Silence

Unless I was flying off the handle
Or something in my hands was,
No one heard me
When I was undermined
I broke and so did things
I threw. I shattered.
Oh. Now you hear me.

Flirting With Satan

You’re really not strong enough
But of course the dull days
Found their way
To uncover boredom streets in your mind

Before a thought has fully hatched
Your soul will have been snatched
He needs but a crack
A crack of a flirtatious smile
That to you was harmless, so it seemed

But before you knew it, you had undressed
The thought patterns that led to manifest corrupt seeds
You see, nothing really happens over night
Unless you were already sleeping with the enemy

That gradual wading into the bay
Will have you waiting
To get saved from the overwhelming waves
And the only lifting you can count on
Is Satan sifting you like wheat

How did you get this far from reality
Without a buoy in sight?
Unsafe practices rolling out left and right

Hoping to wedge your way in between those hips
Praying for no hedge of protection to penetrate those lips
That tempting rush of doing what's wrong
Will have you thinking it’s her that you're flirting with
Silly you, you're flirting with Satan.

Ms. Warden

When did these roles reverse?!
It seems the generations that preceded me had more time.
More time to nurse
More time to rehearse
Their individual life roles
Before they started to thwart
Themselves into this twilight zone.

I had not yet hit an opportunity for a quarter life crisis
When life as I knew it had shifted.
Wait….this was my crisis. Not knowing the game,
I rolled the dice and I was a winner.
My prize?
I became a single parent to a senior. Citizen, that is.

The package includes overseeing all things.
First, just translation.
Then came the mortgage and primary source of transportation.
Sprinkle in balancing of checkbooks,
Medication management and enforcement,
PhDs in movements and dis-ease
No longer planning trips as I please.

Outlay of menus is required.
Self-care is hard to fit in but needed to maintain the fire.
My pitcher stays on "refill please"
To keep pouring into them even though I'm always tired.
I'm over to cook breakfast to make sure dad eats.
Fifteen years later, this is progressive
Except that word is absolutely deceptive.

The reality is that now I have two
And I have to remind myself daily
That it's not that "I have to…"
It's that "I get to…" and that "I'm blessed to…"
Even when I'm feeling defeated.

I'm celebrating what I've won.
I am the one.
The one that gets to capture the memories,

The laughs
The walks to the park,
The good nights where I tuck them in in the dark,
The not so good days where I play mom and try my best to figure it all out
The video recordings of stories of them in their prime.
I am the one that gets the most out of their time.
Ms. Warden gets to ride until the end of the line.

Bettie Rubble

I've tried to take rocks out of your sinking ship,
But you steadily haul them back in,
As if it's not enough to lug around the weights that you carry within.

When I die, you'll need to find someone else to blame.
Funny how I'm at the center of everything
Yet your problems existed before you even knew my name.

I've extended my hand to you day and night,
Left work and school for this shhhhh,
But even that causes for you to pick a fight

It's easier to place fault on others.
I've done it, I know.
Analyze for a second. How far are you willing to go?

Why did I even ask?
Slandering my dead brother?
Yes, the one you never even met.

I'll be patient waaay over here.
Just a suggestion, those rocks stack better
When the foundation is clear.

Custodian's Closet

I answered to your every beck and call
Despite our differences I was there through it all

I allowed to be sucked into your dysfunctional whirlwind
All the garbage, I gathered it and held it in

There was never any regard for my well being
Left and right, I got called on to scrub everything

The free ride is over. You have to clean up your own mess
I can no longer pacify you at my expense

I put away my broom. It will sweep no more, no less
I wish you luck with your life experience

Resolutions

Resolutions, I keep searching for some
But my demons tell me that there are none
They've convinced me to become the invisible girl
The girl that no one would care for in this world

They've made things so daunting to face
I feel as if I'm virtually running in place
I want to progress
But my demons keep my mind in the past, my mind cannot rest

Can't rest with the thoughts in my head pacing
Back in forth so fast that my blood starts racing
I get so hot that I nearly burst into flames
I'm on the brink of going insane

So many things that I keep inside of myself
Pen and paper have made me a master of stealth
Built up resentment has made me corrupt
And caused my anger to explode like when volcanoes erupt

In a world full of people, feeling so alone
Accepting to be walked on as long as I could call the footprint my own

Assessment & Plan

Finding Myself

How could I just be me?
Didn't know what that meant
Didn't even know who I was
So weekly I saw a therapist,
Entered the same room
And created a different fuss

He guided me to the shallow edge
Yet I found myself drowning in painful memories
Neck deep in a pool made of tears
Recalling wounds that had never healed
Lacerations I thought I hid from the world
Some that I hid even from myself for so many years

I walked through life feeling magnified
Under heavy scrutiny
Feeling followed by an evil eye
Everyone was out to get me
I didn't know how I'd get by

Indirectly taught to serve
I was to be seen, not heard
Unworthy of a voice, I began to believe
I became a shadow
After these messages I perceived

Not believing in myself
Paranoia had set in much like rigor mortis on the dead
I buried myself into it and it became my truth
Scared to speak on it
I didn't know how
Filth exploded out of my mouth when I did, expecting my pain to soothe

Recipes for cynicism, I had them all
Feeling measly in the eyes of my family
Feeling minute in my own eyes
Weary of the world and everyone in it
Cooking in a pessimistic vortex
Blind to any good, all the raised patterns spelled lies

No one could be trusted
All held ulterior motives, I was sure
Eager to please, while simultaneously feeling used
Confusion stormed about
I couldn't tell up from down
The lines were blurred between love and abuse

When being told I "had to" do something
I felt under attack
A jab to my injured self esteem
I couldn't piece it together
Why was it my job?
I was being singled out, it seemed

There's no one to blame
My experiences, I can not change
But the way I regard them can
Wrongfully internalized
I compared treatment to value
It doesn't correlate, I'm beginning to understand

Once weak, sad and unstable
Engulfed in rage
I learned that circumstances don't have to be different
For me to begin evolving
So I eagerly sample footing out of this mental cage

Each week I drop a grain of sand
A few grains with each verse
Finding clarity in writing
I'm feeling so much better now
Love, confidence, hope
Even strength to start shining

I like who I'm becoming
I'm starting to grow out of this shell
The options are clear and it's me I choose
I'm unveiling a beautiful statue
It once lay under a ton of debris
Now it's the debris that looks like a sad excuse

Self-realization; it’s a beautiful gift
Even when what we discover is not so nice
It grants us the opportunity to reflect on ourselves
Over a hundred therapy weeks behind me
Probably a hundred more before me
Despite the time, I’m closer to finding myself

Happy New Year

As the year comes to an end
I'm reminded of my wondrous friend
His patience, love and ability to mend
A broken heart...a broken spirit

Just hours away from a new year
Moments away from fireworks and cheer
Don't let the noise of the world block your ability to hear
His voice calling you by name

If you need a new year's resolution try realizing your worth
He came here to die for YOU on this earth
He gave us an opportunity to live eternally through a second birth
Talk about a new year… talk about a new you

Let's focus on the real celebration reasons
He remains the same no matter what the season
He forgives all, protects all and loves all. No one like our Jesus
Happy new year

Examination Room

I never thought that a fear so great would push me to decide
To confront myself. From me, I could no longer hide.
That day I walked in and threw my demons on the table.
Tears overflowing, body shivering, physical pain, anything but stable.
I opened up too many wounds at once and created my own category 6 disaster.
It seemed too late to slow down, my initial momentum kept my mind spinning faster and faster.
Nightmares kept me dreading sleep.
I kid you not, I was on the verge of defeat.
So far, I've learned that it's harder to keep running.
It's clearer now that through foggy tears, happiness is the outcome.
It is no lie, I've merely just begun to know myself, my life, my flaws.
Each day moving forward to love and accept it all.
Embracing even the jagged edges that cut so deep
I've accepted them, but that doesn't mean they no longer make me weep
I'm making it through simply because He delivers on "I will never leave nor forsake thee"
It was through Him I began crafting with the tools provided to me.
Walking into volatile grounds, phase one.
Pray hard for strength not to turn back, the pain has just begun.
Make some sense of the torment, phase two.
"It gets worse before it gets better" never felt so true
What I feel now is determination, this must be phase three.
Whatever steps follow, I can taste it, they set me free.
Final phase, I strap on my armour and aim to admire
Myself in the mirror, as this sculpture is coming to be, from walking through fire.

Restoration

Splintered edges and rusty hinges
She had taken as much as she could handle
The storm had beaten her tirelessly
Day in and day out, the entire house in shambles

Her foundation was crumbling
Powerful wind gusts rocked her side to side
The torment continued
There was nowhere to hide

The dark clouds would momentarily retreat
Allowing enough sunlight to crack her boards
Although the weather granted breaks
It seemed to be just enough to prepare for more

Storm after storm she became ragged
Eventually they were too much to bear
Her exterior began to break and fall
Rotting from all the wear and tear

After all she had endured
She was not ready for her demise
She began to creak often
As if pleading for help through discreet cries

Lone behold, that's all she needed
Help soon was on the way
Tools began to arrive
As soon as the following day

The rebuilding began
New bolts secured her foundation
Damaged boards were smashed out
The pain continued throughout her transformation

Her splintered surface smoothed over
It's amazing what a little sanding can do
And with a touch of sealant
She shined just like new

Old watermarks are still visible on her surface
No longer provoking feelings of void
They remind her of her endurance
The journey now brings her joy

It took nearly an entire breakdown
To learn appreciation through depreciation
You may crumble down to your last limb
But never lose focus on the healing found in restoration

Soloist

She doesn't pray for a man. However good, he will not bring her through
To fill the void or change what her mind brings her to

Of prince charming she will not dream
Because it is not he that will solve these things

The strength must be hers to push off of land & set sail
Through the choppy waters of everything that makes her ail

How does she request help when smiles adorn the surface of her skin
On the inside lives a different story, emotions wearing her thin

Self-love, just one of her innermost battles; a tough battle she must endure
Looking to the sky for answers. Please God, help renew her

They say pray for your enemies and keep them near
But she is her worst enemy and she brings herself to fear

She keeps taking the trial into her own shaky hands
Although this has proven every time to crash land

Relax and be patient you'll see
Time will aid you in getting where you need to be

Bikram

I walk in confident
Focusing on my breath
Quickly glistening with sweat
My heart is pounding
My breathing is getting deeper
My body is trembling
My muscles are burning
Sweat beads are rolling down my spine
I give it my all
It feels like hours
Contorting my body
I feel strong
I am in control
In the end, I lay there
Motionless. Eyes closed. Satisfied

Dear Sunday

Dear Sunday,

I used to dread you
You taunted me
The weekend was over
My rest had come to an end
You reminded me of my early rise for the next workday

But boy have you redeemed yourself

It was a Sunday that I met an interesting gentleman
It was a Sunday that I heard his praising songs
It was a Sunday that I discovered his religious servitude
It was a Sunday that we established our relationship
It was a Sunday that he hugged my tears away in his arms
It was a Sunday that I met his entire family
It was a Sunday that we shared our first kiss
It was a Sunday that I heard him utter "I love you"

Now Sunday, how will you ever top this?

Two of a Kind

Apple juice lovers
Black preludes
Right placement of birthmarks

Sensitive brown skin
Sleep deprived writers
Quirky remarks

Contagious smiles
Matching dimples
To diffuse is their goal

Dead set humor
Total of four left feet
God bless their souls

Long nail beds
Similar blind eyes
Equally evil laughs

Angelic at first glance
Mischievous at the second
Dramatization is only the half

Exceptional barber
Special stylist
No ordinary cuts for their curly hair

Serious about food
Don't mess with their sleep,
Snacks and especially not the gummy bears!

Preference of cubed ice
We need our meats
If we can't use our hands, we'll use our toes

Creative genes
Always in tune
Oh so glad they got rid of that baggy clothes

Awful actors
Bad poker faces
But both ready for this plight
Two drops of kindness
An ounce of love
A dash of compassion
A pinch of patience and thoughtfulness
Just a hint of crazy
Step back. Together they ignite

Side Effects

Temptation

Fire truck red
Lips
Big Sur voluptuous waves
Hips
Utter her name
Call
Piercing brown eyes
Doll

Flowing down to the waist
Hair
Light finger tips touch
Snare
Sensitive, soft, smooth
Skin
Battle your thoughts
Sin

Quiet, calm, romantic
Atmosphere
Polite array of words
Sincere
Hand placed at the small of her back
Enticing
Building up to the moment
Exciting

Closeness of his body
Torment
Warmth of his breath
Enjoyment
Flirtatious crooked smile
Manipulation
Nervousness setting in
Hesitation

Body temperatures rising
Mild
Thousands of thoughts racing
Wild

Lean in for a kiss
Surrender
Berry stained lips
Splendor

Flaming internal desires
Presence
Walking away from temptation
Essence

Your Arrival

The day has just begun
I've already thought about you more than once
The days have quickly turned to nights, weeks, months

How long will I wait?
They say patience is a virtue
So I keep doing me, until the moment that I meet you

Mild sighs escape my lips
Hearts are difficult to attain
On the mere thought of having yours, I will sustain

So close yet so far
I can almost feel you at my fingertips
So I close my eyes and play pretend that you are closer than this

Moonlight shines
Night stars adorn the sky
Casting wishes upon them, that you are THAT guy

Always on time
I'm practicing my shots in the dark
I can hardly wait to discover who you arc

How long must I wait to meet you?

Black Siren II

Can you hear the silent song
My body is playing
To call you near?

If you can, listen closely
As the tone is set
By the rhythm of my breath

Like crashing waves
I'm splashing on your pier
Chest to chest I can feel

The drumming sounds
Of your heart setting the pace
For your rocking

Gliding your fingertips across my body
Searching for the perfect keystroke
Creating sensuous notes
All the while lips locking

Swaying like palm trees
Are the movements of this conductor
Giving rise to perfect harmony in this duet
No need to rush
Take your time plucking the chords
Fine tuning this instrument

There is no special form
Not quite a specific rhyme
Just about the perfect pitch
For this beautiful melody

Embracing the highs and lows
The contours and ranges
Not worried about sequence
Just preparing for an exceptional finale.

The Sequel

Alluring vibrations
Draw him near
Every detail, he's willing to learn

She's elusive
Yet receptive to his plan
Perhaps she will love & learn

Earning trust
Making his presence & intentions known
Mouthing her sweet siren song

Awakening senses
Embracing her firmly
Rocking her rhythmically in his arms

Nervous palpitations
As he takes her hand in his
She pleads, "Don't ever let go."

Dream state
The state to find her
Where she goes, he must go

Tested the waters
He knows she's ready
Boldly exclaiming, "Be mine black siren!"
Looking forward to forever and a day.

The Last Day

Plumes of smoke fill the air
As my heart is charred, I continually stare
At the ceiling with a knot in my throat.
I swallow hard as my OB tells me that you are not there.

You appear to have drowned
As you ever so slightly sway.
I see you but I don't hear a sound.
This is... by far...the worst day
Of my life.

Everyone is at home expecting a gender reveal.
Meanwhile, I silently lay.
I dare not open my mouth
As a second doctor is called in to confirm this ordeal.

COVID! If only I could exchange your existence for my baby's.
My husband could not be here,
So that we could get lost together in each other's silence
As our emotions plummet off of our faces in the form of tears.

The reality was I was stuck with Dr. Farastoo
And her apology "Because of this virus, I can't even hug you.
Get dressed, I'll come back and discuss what to do."

Storm clouds are building in my eyes.
I quickly texted my crew.
Having not digested the size of the news,
Not softening the blow, I hit send on "Our baby has died."

An awkward silence followed
The receipt of my options which I didn't really hear.
I wanted to leave, I'm sure it was clear.
She invited me for a video chat the next day.

As I waited alone for my visit deets,
I paced in the room in a sad attempt to isolate thoughts.
Before anything became clear,
The floodgates broke. Except it wasn't water.
A massive amount of blood was oozing to my feet.

Like anaphylaxis, my throat was on lock.
I looked down the hall for someone to help
And conjured up barely above a whisper, "Excuse me."
The Medical Assistant recognized the look on my face.
She bolted in with pads and pain meds to take.

This is so unreal as I type.
Honey, I need you. I need clothes. Come get me please.
"Take a few deep breaths" I tell myself
As I'm dialing up Mom to tell her about our baby.

Stephen must have run every red light to get to me.
As he's cleaning me up, my in-laws are driving down.
We pull up at home to find my dad outside distraught and in disbelief.

Is this what it feels like when the world is ending?
The only traces of your existence are smears.
Smears of blood,
Congratulations cards replaced by cards of sympathy for my departed and beloved.

Our bed looks painfully flat.
Beds are supposed to be that way, right?
I had become accustomed to the pillows used for propping me up at night.
All that previously reminded me of you was tucked clear out of sight.

Wondering if there is anything strong enough to sedate me.
Being cautious about pleading for God to just take me.
I attempt to make it right in my heart
That the reason you had to abruptly depart
Was because of a mistake in the factory.
Yes, you've gone because you were one but you were meant to be two.

Baby Sharpe, we love and miss you.

Recovery

Courage

Wanting to run before I crawl
The flesh on my knees is bloody raw
I am no longer afraid to fall
Although the pain may cause a scream

Coddling my voice until I am ready to sing
Learning to pamper my injured wings
Inviting the darkness of evening
I welcome the night, I am ready to dream

Today I wake and I am ready to fly
Searching for novel things in novel skies
Refocusing the lens on these glossy eyes
Sometimes things aren't as hard as they seem

On My Way

Putting an end to senseless lamentation
Deflecting useless frustration
Currently building on a sturdy foundation

Brushing off the fingers pointing blame
Learning to enjoy the beauty of rain
Meditating on peace to stay sane

Leaving behind the worldly and absurd
Searching for truth in what I've heard
Focusing daily on the good word

Practicing the art of self control
Working diligently to reach my goals
Happy is the state of my mind and soul

So there will be no more slammed doors
And no more despair seeping from my pores
If you listen closely, you may hear my inner lioness roar

Powerful Might

Waves roar out in his lecture

Our minds burst open and ingest it like second nature

His views flow off of lips in a scrupulous fashion

Not for one second dismissing an ounce of his passion

Vivid is the torch that ignites that bold tone

The tone that assures frightened folks that they don't stand alone

There's a smoothness in the delivery of his innermost expression

It makes three hour class feel like a brief session

Vibes flow like a breeze with powerful might

Like solid fists ready to throw blows for peace in our lives

Excitement silently seeps through our veins

Ecstatic about today's movements and all of its gains

His tongue delivers a message solid like roots in the ground

But as long as the fire in our eyes burns, there's no need for sound

Don't stop organizing, don't stop what you preach

Keep your flame exposed and more lives you will reach

Love Resuscitation

This year we've known each other for half of our lives.
Fifteen years. It's surreal how time flies.
Throughout the years you've been there to shine light on the dark things that I've been through.
For all of your support, I truly thank you.
You've demonstrated huge efforts to keep me from walking away.
Hindsight, I wouldn't have it any other way.
You stuck by me beyond my trials and showed true loyalty.
You've proven to be patient, loving, kind, non-ordinary.
Your positivity has helped me with so many things.
You're living proof that angels walk amongst human beings.
The care we draw out of each other goes to show me,
that we own nurturing souls. Identical. Exactly.
Our bond overshadowed the days in which you were my high school crush.
Focusing more on how throughout separate relationships we kept in touch.
I remember vividly the times in which movie previews we critiqued
and how good it felt to share the friendship we both seeked.
I recall watching movies, arms intertwined.
Nothing beyond this ever crossed my mind.
Until recent years, I began to back track over a decade of your genuine affection.
All the qualities in you, I noted, made for a much stronger connection.
It was as if a veil was lifted from my eyes.
It was romance that I felt, I was starting to realize.
So many times you held me in a gentle embrace.
All this time my ideal man was staring me in the face.
I never imagined that you would fill me in such a way.
The feelings snuck up on me as quickly as night turns to day.
A fantasy drew us closer, until one day we kissed.
Complete tenderness is what I found in those lips.
It comes as no question why our encounters are so sensuous.
We polarize with raw emotion, pure sentiment.
Your passionate caress causes my cup to overflow,
Spilling over your body. I can go without telling; you already know.
You and me together, we can create the eighth wonder.
The possibilities are endless each time we take this further.
I'm entangled in your web and I don't want to escape.
Eyes closed as I indulge in the thought of your face.

His & Hers

He listens intently to her words
"**I** love you" she whispers
Softly taking his hand

How patiently they've waited for this moment
Elated to finally become one flesh
Rendering it all to each other
Say I do

Ex-Factor

My knight
Meek,
Brilliant, patient
You are excellence.

I Do

When I thought about
What words I'd say in my vows
I thought it'd probably be best to write them out

My words through conversation
Are shaky at best
So I wrote this poem instead
To set my mind to rest

I think back to our first hangouts
Dinner, movies, boxing, take out
Laughing as I could literally see
Your devious thoughts as they swarmed about

For months I made sure
To keep you at bay
Silly of me to think a
Bridge or two would keep you away

So I decided to lay truth out on the table
Although much harder than to tell you a lie
I unveiled my faults, fears and failures
So you'd know what you had to get through,
Whom you had to stand by

And despite all of that, day in and day out
New interactions took place
And with every single opportunity
You never failed to put a smile on my face

You accepted my broken pieces
And brought forth yours
Our shattered pieces lay like bricks together
Creating new paths, new journeys leading to new doors

Each day I spend with you
I see positive changes, I see growth
I see a real desire to improve
In you and I both

Really, I'm thankful
Happy about how things unfolded
Knowing without a doubt it was
God's plan, God's timing on how well we together molded

From today onward, I am no longer
Just your friend
I transition to your filler of blanks, slice of pie
Your lover 'til the very end

As I feel my heart skip a beat,
I notice yours takes two
I guess that's just a reminder that you'll make up where I am weak
As I will do the same for you.
Stephen Sharpe, I love you

Made in the USA
Middletown, DE
31 July 2022